THE
FESTIVE FOOD
OF
RUSSIA

Lesley Chamberlain

ILLUSTRATED BY SALLY MALTBY

KYLE CATHIE LIMITED

First published 1996 by
Kyle Cathie Limited
20 Vauxhall Bridge Road, London SW1V 2SA

Copyright © 1996 Lesley Chamberlain
Illustrations copyright © 1996 Sally Maltby

ISBN 1 85626 195 6

Colour origination by Colour Symphony Pte Ltd,
Singapore
Printed by Chromo Litho, Italy

Contents

Introduction

Orthodox Christianity, with its strict insistence on an annual pattern of feasts and fasts, long ago shaped Russian eating into a pattern of extremes. For more than 200 days a year, divided into seven fasts, the faithful were not allowed to consume meat and dairy products. These Church rules were widely kept, and particularly before and after the Great Fast of Lent, which also prohibited fish, the feasting continued for days to compensate.

The religious impetus has all but disappeared today, but the extremes remain. With a conflicting array of native and European-style dishes the Russian table is both frugal and lavish. The humblest soups and the grandest fish and pork dishes together mark special occasions.

By the early eighteenth century the Tsars and the aristocracy were cultivating extravagant French tastes, for which both chefs and ingredients had to be imported. The Empress Anna Ivanovna, who came to the throne in 1730, had a French chef called Formay and, by the time of Catherine the Great 50 years later, Gallic habits were highly desirable in the kitchens of the rich. In the 1820s no less a gastronomic artist than Antoine Carême was cooking for the Alexander I in the so-called 'northern Venice' of St Petersburg.

The French ushered in a culinary revolution. The magnificent fish of the Russian rivers, sturgeon and sterlet, pike and perch, always a crowning glory of the table, acquired a new finish when they were poached in white wine and laced with crayfish. The fine fish pie, *kulebyaka*, was Frenchified with salmon and puff pastry, though its native form was splendid. Unleavened pastry, sweet cream, olive oil and béchamel sauce all became part of the modern

8

Russian repertoire. White bread appeared alongside the more robust rye loaves of common custom. Tomatoes, lemons and pineapples brought a new natural brightness and freshness to a table which for much of the year traditionally relied on pickles for its colour and its vitamin C. This was the European Russian cuisine which the characters of Leo Tolstoy's novels enjoyed at their banquets.

Yet Tolstoy's characters sometimes got bored with the grand culinary manner. At times they would slink away and relish a bowl of Russian porridge (*kasha*) or a jar of salted mushrooms from the countryside instead, and their divided appetites expressed a fundamental split in Russian tastes. A fondness for simple native dishes like fermented cabbage soup (*shchi*), meat and fish pies, buckwheat, mushrooms in sour cream, sweet pies and buns stuffed with curd cheese, and honey cakes, was never supplanted. French-Russian food celebrated affluence, simple Russian food celebrated Russia.

To this base of Russian and Russian-French cooking modern cooks have added an enthusiasm for recipes from Central Asia and the Caucasus, and held on to a few old ideas from the Russian Far East.

Political upheavals and economic hardship have meanwhile encouraged a cuisine of legendary generosity. It is never more apparent than on the special days of the calendar to which this book is devoted.

Maslenitsa

BUTTERWEEK

By the mid-nineteenth century, the week before the harsh Orthodox regime of Lent had become the second most spectacular occasion in the gastronomic calendar. The Russian equivalent of Mardi Gras combined rich feasting with fun at the fairground; glamorous troika trips over frozen rivers and helter-skelter tobogganing. In seventeenth-century St Petersburg, Tsar Peter, the city's founder, opened proceedings on the Monday by riding with his officers on the swings. Many of the events would take place beside the river Neva. Each day of the week-long festival had its particular character. Stravinsky's highly decorative, theatrical ballet, *Petrushka,* evokes all the colour and merriment of the now vanished *Maslenitsa* festival.

The food was a celebration of winter preserves and the products of the Russian fisheries. The food rules, originally a step towards the coming fast because of the exclusion of meat, were quickly interpreted as a chance to binge on cream and fish, lavishly sandwiched between pancakes (*blini*). *Blini* were counted by the elbow and tales abounded of pancake-eating competitions – and the sometimes mortal consquences of over-indulgence.

Blini

Butterweek was lost to the twentieth century because its religious and merchant origins were incompatible with Communism. But *blini* remain as one of the most successful food ideas that the West has ever borrowed from Russia. They date back to pagan times, when a pancake was offered to the dead on the Sunday preceding Shrovetide. In Christian Russia they became staples of both the restricted and the lavish table. When Russia's most famous culinary name, Eliza Molokhovets, wrote the bible of Russian bourgeois cooking, *A Gift for Young Housewives*, in the 1870s, she included seven different recipes.

The essential ingredient, buckwheat flour, distinguishes *blini* from a bland French *crêpe*. Buckwheat has the gutsy flavour of smoke and earth, and a muddy colour which perfectly offsets white cream and the gleaming orange colour of salmon caviare or pinky orange smoked salmon. The finest grade of smooth and speckled buckwheat flour is justly named after silk

The most familiar size for *blini* is about 12.5cm/5in across, the size of a tea plate. Traditionally *blini* were baked in cast iron saucers. A small heavy iron frying pan lightly oiled gives the best modern results.

The usual leavening of yeast or, less traditionally, baking powder, gives *blini* a thicker, spongier texture than white flour pancakes. In the Russian way *blini* may therefore be served unfolded. Most important are the accompaniments: something fishy, a generous dollop of sour cream and a glass of ice-cold vodka. Salmon or sturgeon caviare are grand ideas. Lumpfish roe is a possible substitute. Modern restaurant chefs favour smoked salmon.

Blini Batter
with added White Flour

Makes 8–10 blini
300g/12oz/1½cups plain white flour
100g/4oz/½cup buckwheat flour
½teaspoon salt
½teaspoon baking powder (or ½teaspoon dried
   yeast, dissolved in 2 tablespoons warm water)
2 eggs, beaten
300ml/½pint/1cup milk or sour milk
sunflower oil for frying
3-4tablespoons chopped spring onions (optional)
sour cream

1 Sieve the flours, salt and baking powder together, add the eggs and the milk and stir to a smooth consistency. Alternatively dissolve the yeast in the warm water and add to the mixture of flour, eggs and milk. Leave to rise in a warm place.
2 To cook *blini*, swill a teaspoon of oil around the warm pan, allow the oil to heat up but not smoke, then test to see if a drop of mixture sizzles. Add mixture to cover pan, cook a few minutes until top side is just firm, turn and cook a minute more.
3 Serve the *blini* either straight from the pan or keep them warm in the oven. Have the fillings ready in advance for people to help themselves, together with a bowl each of spring onion and sour cream.

   Onion and cream bring out the flavours at a table where lemon juice is not a common accompaniment to fish. They also add texture. Russian sour cream, *smetana*, is a cultured product akin to crème fraîche and Polish *smatana*. Other 'sour creams' in their full fat versions are perfectly acceptable, only heavy and a little bland.

Traditional Bliní Batter

These dark, strong-flavoured pancakes are more airy and crumbly than their workaday counterparts. Their especially gritty taste seems to have been invented to complement sour cream and smoked salmon, and the delicate texture and genuinely unusual combination of flavours easily outweigh the slight difficulty in handling a mixture that can stick to the pan. The use of yeast as a leaven maximizes the lightness. An hour in normal conditions should suffice for the batter to rise.

Makes 8–10 bliní
½teaspoon yeast
500ml/¾pint/2cups water
350g/12oz/1½cups buckwheat
   flour
500ml/¾pint/2cups milk
pinch salt
1-2 eggs, beaten

1 Dissolve the yeast in half a cup of the warm water. Scald the flour with the remaining water heated to boiling point and mix to remove any lumps. When just warm add the yeast mixture and leave to rise.
2 Add the milk, salt and eggs. Leave to rise again before using.

The Coming of Spring

Effigies of the Old Year, in the form of straw dolls, were sometimes burnt during Butterweek. The writer Alexei Tolstoy compared the roundness of *blini* to the roundness of the sun, suggesting they were a pagan midwinter evocation of warm days which would eventually return. But in Russia Spring has always been a long time coming, and the seven-week Lenten fast did not hasten it. Small compensation, if a precious winged sign of Spring's arrival appeared, was to fashion plain pastry into fanciful shapes. These *zhavaronki*, or larks, became traditional on March 9th.

Zhavaronki

LARKS

¼ teaspoon dried yeast
2 tablespoons sugar
450g/1lb/2 cups flour
180ml/⅓ pint/¾ cup water
3 eggs, beaten, plus 1 for brushing finished 'larks'
2 tablespoons melted butter or oil
pinch of salt
a few currants for decoration

1   Dissolve the yeast and the sugar in the warm water, mix in the sifted flour and salt, add the 3 eggs and the melted butter and knead to a smooth dough. Leave to rise till double in bulk.
2   Twist into 6 or more plaits, cross over the ends of each plait, forming the bird's head at one end, studded with a currant for an eye, and the tail at the other, patterned with a fork. Leave to rise again.
3   Brush with beaten egg and bake in a hot oven (200°C/400°F/gas 6) for 10-15 minutes. Serve these plain buns with other cakes and Russian tea.

Easter

The Resurrection of Christ, ending the seven-week Lenten fast (*Veliky Post*), is spiritually the most momentous and moving event in the Orthodox calendar. A tall, yeast-leavened cake, *kulich*, the shape of an Orthodox priest's hat, used to be baked and placed before the iconostasis the week before Easter. Every day the faithful would process with it round the Church. After midnight on Easter Sunday it would be divided among the congregation to eat in celebration of Christ's rebirth. People would also take the family *kulich* to the church for the priest to bless. Per pound of flour *kulich* might contain up to 18 eggs to signify the richness of the event.

Once the family returned from church the feasting would begin. A table of the richest foods, with this towering cake at its centre, stood both as a token of renewed Christian faith and a chance for family and friends to indulge. Best clothes were worn and the finest lace-trimmed tablecloth laid on the table. Flavoured vodkas glinted in their transparent bottles. Eggs transformed into objects of the most delicate folk art were heaped in wooden bowls. A red flower decorated the top of the *kulich*, which was dramatically iced down a third of its length in sugar and eggwhite.

Inevitably in a small community the priest would call by during the day to sample the cooking. This would also include a whole sucking pig, a dish of a whole fish or chicken in aspic, and a pyramid of moulded sweet cheese imprinted with the Cyrillic letters XB, signifying *Xristos voskres* (Christ is Risen!).

Kulich
YEAST-LEAVENED CAKE

½teaspoon dried yeast
300ml/½pint/1cup milk
700g/1½lb/3cups flour
6 egg yolks
¼teaspoon salt
1teaspoon vanilla essence
75g/3oz/½cup raisins soaked in brandy
150g/5oz butter
120g/4oz/½cup sugar

For the glaze
120g/4oz/½cup icing sugar
1 egg white, beaten stiff
few drops of vanilla essence

1   Dissolve the yeast in the warm milk and knead
into the flour. Mix the remaining ingredients
together, then beat into the flour mixture.
2   Grease and flour 2 identical baking tins 12cm/5in
in diameter. The mixture evenly divided between
the 2 should reach no higher than a half to two-
thirds the height. Leave the cakes to rise in a warm
place until they reach the top of the tin.
3   Bake in a preheated oven (180°C/350°F/gas 4)
until golden and cooked through. After 35 minutes
lower the heat to 160°C/325°F/gas 3 and bake for
another 25 minutes or until the cakes are done. The
sign is that a skewer will emerge clean. If the cakes
are darkening on top during baking, cover with foil.
4   Unmould carefully and cool on a wire rack. Place
the cakes one on top of the other and glaze down to
the divide.
5   Wrap in tin foil until required. Kulich is a rich
cake which will easily keep for 10 days. Any dryness
is offset by the richness of the *paskha* spread upon it
(see p.18).

Paskha

In Soviet cookbooks this lovely mixture of cream and curd cheese, cake spices and dried fruit traditionally bearing the Russian name for Easter, was reduced to being called 'a mass of cheese'. In the minds of both believers and non-believers, however, it never lost the significance it possessed on the ninteenth-century table when fashioned for Easter Sunday morning in beautiful wooden moulds. These gave the imprint not only of the 2 Cyrillic letters betokening the Resurrection, but also of the Orthodox Cross with its distinctive 2 horizontals. Once the side-hinged pyramid was removed, the *paskha* was sometimes decorated with a piped, coloured cream border and a flower set on top.

120g/4oz/½cup cream cheese
120g/4oz/½cup curd cheese
1tablespoon sour cream
2tablespoons icing sugar
1tablespoon grated lemon peel
2tablespoons candied fruit to taste

1   Mix the cheeses and cream and suspend in a muslin bag or a paper filter for 24 hours in the refrigerator to allow any excess liquid to drain off.
2   Mix the drained cheese with the sugar, lemon peel and candied fruit; mould into a pyramid and decorate. Glacé cherries add a wonderful touch of colour. Slivers of toasted almond may also be included in the *paskha* or used to embellish the exterior.

Decorated Eggs

The tradition of painting eggs is known throughout the Christian world. But in no other country did it become such a great art as in Russia, thanks to the fabulous work of Karl Gustavovich Fabergé, born in St Petersburg in 1846. A fine craftsman, he achieved worldwide fame when, moving away from jewellery into objects of fantasy, he acquired a commission from Tsar Alexander III to make an Easter Egg for the Danish-born Tsarina, Marie Feodorovna. That first Imperial egg, made in 1884, had a shell of gold-enamelled white opaque that was polished to give the effect of a hen's egg. It contained a yellow, sand-blasted gold yolk, and inside the yolk was a golden hen. The hen contained a diamond replica of the Imperial Crown.

Fabergé in his decorative art achieved that balance which Russian cuisine also wished to attain as it came of age at the end of the Tsarist Empire. The tradition was Russian, and this cosmopolitan master craftsman transformed it with luxury materials and the delicacy of genius into a high art. The result delighted the world.

Barents Sea.

NORWAY

SWEDEN

FINLAND

Baltic Sea.

St. Petersburg

River Ob

R. Don

Moscow

linsk

R. Volga

Samara

dessa

Rostov

Volgograd.

lack
ea

Astrakhan.

Omsk

Caspian Sea

Aral
Sea

Arctic Circle.

R.Lena

• Yakutsk

Lake
Baikal

Jouosibirsk

• Irkutsk

Land below 600ft.
Land above 600ft.
Land below sea·level.

0   500 m.
       500 kms.

Vodka

There cannot be a Russian celebration without it. The name, sometimes fondly referred to as *vodochka*, means 'little water', and much recent scholarship has gone into proving its world origins are Russian from the fifteenth century.

The Orthodox Church encouraged vodka in preference to beer and wine, for these were linked to continuing pagan festivals whereas vodka was non-religious and timeless. A long history of state control of vodka production is thought by some to underscore the closeness of vodka to the national soul. The Tsar bestowed subsidized vodka traditionally 'by the bucket' and at least in 50ml/¼pint/¼cup on his humble and obedient children. The high quality reassured the people of the sovereign's goodwill in times of trouble.

The way the pure Russian spirit is produced, ideally diluted with the soft water of Russian forest streams and filtered through birch charcoal, offers an alternative account of vodka's place in the national psyche. The water itself is neither distilled nor boiled.

To say that 'Russian vodka possesses a special smoothness and softness, since the water in it is not soulless but living,' is one poetic view. The newly distilled spirit enters its first symbolic process of purification by undergoing the Russian winter. When traditionally made it was rapidly cooled by being set outside in the winter cold. Distilled at its best from rye grain, which grows so well in Russia's cold northern soil (though potatoes have been used in hard times), Russian vodka has a distinctive taste. The flavour accrues from a judicious addition in small quantities of other grains such as barley, buckwheat, oats and wheat. Woodland herbs, young buds of Russian trees (birch, willow, pussy-willow), leaves (cherry and blackcurrant) and foreign spices also enhance the taste and the national character of the drink. Its consumption neat, in round after round of speeches and tributes, is the most famous aspect of Russian sociability and diplomacy worldwide. The idea of diluting it Western-style with mixers constitutes for Russians a special kind of sacrilege.

Russia's foremost contemporary vodka expert, William Pokhlebkin, a moderate man with an encyclopedic knowledge of Russian gastronomy, accepts that many ordinary Russians prefer to drink vodka 'not sitting at a table but holding on to a lamppost'. But he hopes his countrymen will eventually come to see sense in moderation. He advocates drinking it a tiny glass at a time with food, which can be zakuski (p.31), blini (p.11) or bread and pickles. For special occasions Russians advocate pshenichnaya vodka, with a high proportion of wheat. The first sign of a cold brings out the pepper vodka (vodka flavoured with a whole red pimento). Lemon vodka is a must over ice cream.

May 1st
and other Public Holidays

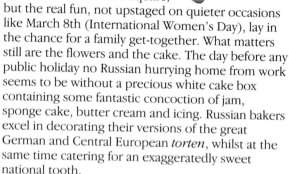

The Soviet public holidays which replaced festive dates on the Church Calendar continue to be occasions for special treats. May 1st (International Labour Day) and November 7th (Revolution Day) brought parades of tanks and smiling workers out on to Red Square, but the real fun, not upstaged on quieter occasions like March 8th (International Women's Day), lay in the chance for a family get-together. What matters still are the flowers and the cake. The day before any public holiday no Russian hurrying home from work seems to be without a precious white cake box containing some fantastic concoction of jam, sponge cake, butter cream and icing. Russian bakers excel in decorating their versions of the great German and Central European *torten*, whilst at the same time catering for an exaggeratedly sweet national tooth.

Cakes for public holidays are invariably bought. Yet the slow revival of interest in home cooking among post-Soviet housewives, better stocked shops and a wave of new recipe books suggest a potential return to home baking. The fondness for a non-native style of sweet, light cake is reflected in this more modest, but quite delicious recipe, which can certainly be made at home. The Russian

24

hallmark is the use of a fat-rich *tvorog* or curd cheese to make the sweet filling.

Pirozhnoe s tvorozhym kremom
CREAM CHEESE AND SOUR CREAM SPONGE CAKE

For the cake
120g/4oz/½cup self-raising flour
1 teaspoon baking powder
pinch of salt
90g/3oz caster sugar
3 eggs
2 tablespoons water
1 teaspoon grated lemon rind

For the filling:
60g/2oz/¼cup cream cheese
60g/2oz/¼cup curd cheese or quark
120g/4oz/½cup icing sugar
2 tablespoons sour cream
a few drops of vanilla essence
icing sugar to dust

1   Sieve together the flour, baking powder and salt, then mix in the caster sugar. Beat together the eggs, water and lemon rind, and combine with the flour mixture, stirring until smooth. Bake in 2 greased and floured sandwich tins for 20 minutes in a preheated oven (180°C/350°F/gas 4) or until light golden brown. Cool on a rack.
2   Combine the soft cheese, icing sugar, sour cream and vanilla essence. Spread over 1 layer of the cake, sandwich together and dust the top layer with icing sugar.
3   Serve with Russian tea or sweet sparkling wine.

Celebrating the Fish Catch

The Easter feast lasted 40 days. Two weeks later a new fast, the *Petrovsky* fast, began for Trinity and lasted to the end of June. The call once again to abstain from meat and dairy products coinciding with the high season for river fishing made May and June ideal times for eating fresh fish.

In the Volga town of Samara the abundant spring catch of bream and sterlet and sturgeon required the whole town to volunteer its labour. The men were paid in fish and vodka for their catch of 'living silver'. The fishing industry celebrated at *Maslenitsa* and on the first Sunday in Trinity, around mid-June.

Today not only the fasting habit but many of the fish too have gone from the great rivers, especially from the much-polluted Volga. Happily the recipes remain. Artificial breeding in Russia and abroad has also made available once again the rich and delicate sterlet.

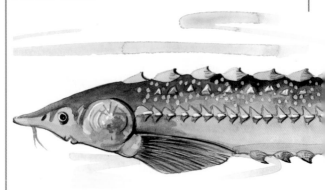

Sterlyad otvarnaya
POACHED STERLET

1 farmed sterlet (*acipenser baeri*) about 2kg/4½lb
2 carrots, roughly chopped
1–2 onions, roughly chopped
bay leaf, black peppercorns
600ml/1pint/2½cups white wine
600ml/1pint/2½cups water
50g/2oz parsley

1 Ask the fishmonger to clean the sterlet, leaving
the magnificent head and tail in place. Put the
vegetables, peppercorns, and seasonings in the
bottom of a fish kettle and pour over the white wine.
Lay the fish on top. Pour over the boiling water,
cover and simmer for 20–25 minutes.
2 If no fish kettle is available wrap the lightly
seasoned sterlet in tin foil and bake it plain in
a preheated oven (180°C/350°F/gas 4).
3 Serve with boiled potatoes. The rich stock may be
used with leftovers to make *ukha* (see p.28*)*.

Ukha

FISHERMAN'S SOUP

Flavoured according to the culinary characteristics of the region, this requires only fresh fish and a well-flavoured fish stock. From the Don this recipe would be made with river fish such as perch and is unusual in containing tomatoes. It may also be made with sea fish.

For the stock:
500-700g/1–1½lb small fish or fish trimmings
1 onion
1 carrot
parsley and parsley root (if available)
1tablespoon sunflower oil
bay leaf, black peppercorns, 1 star anise
salt to taste

For the ukha:
225g/½lb very ripe red tomatoes
450g/1lb sea or river white fish fillet (according to what is used for stock)
fresh parsley and coriander or dill, chopped

1   Cover the fish trimmings or fish trimmings with water and bring to the boil. Skim off scum and simmer for 20 minutes. Strain, reserving liquid.
2   Chop the vegetables fine, soften gently in the oil, add the fish broth and the seasonings. Simmer for 20 minutes.
3   Make 4 knife knicks in the tomatoes and plunge them into boiling water for 30 seconds, then cool; peel and chop.
4   Just before serving, add the fish in bite-size pieces to the simmering stock, then add the tomatoes. Simmer for a few minutes, garnish with fresh greenery, taste for seasoning and serve.

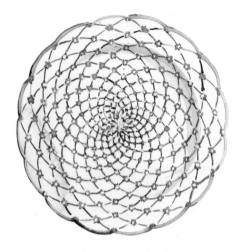

Banquets and Restaurants

Russians love eating out. Through the Communist years this was one pleasure which remained accessible to all and, though the food was not always good, the occasion was memorable, often with a live dance band beating out a quickstep or foxtrot. Public banquets followed much the same menu, without the music.

A typical modern menu would begin with a range of appetizing small dishes called *zakuski*. Main dishes such as the internationally known and much imitated beef *stroganov* and chicken *kiev* would follow. The sweet course would best comprise ice cream and berries. Revellers in style would round off the evening with chocolates and Russian champagne.

Zakuski

RUSSIAN STARTERS

These, inspired by the Nordic cold table, offer informal but luxurious hospitality. Ice-cold vodka accompanies them. Preparation time is short, and can be even shorter with a visit to the delicatessen to buy caviare, cheese, charcuterie and various salted and pickled preserves.

In Moscow the emporium for *zakuski* purchases is Yeliseev's. The two high-ceilinged, flamboyantly decorated, turn-of-the-century food halls are an Aladdin's Cave in Moscow's main street, Tverskoi Boulevard. Ruched white silk blinds, marble counters and white-overalled staff in unusual flat black hats create an unforgettable atmosphere. A spectacle of colossal chandeliers, intricate white and bronze plasterwork and decorated mirrors delights the always dense crowd of shoppers. Fruit cordial gleams pink and orange from glass carbuoys. Wet ewe's milk cheese (*brynza*) and curd cheese (*tvorog*) rise in enticing white blocks and mounds from the dairy slabs. Sausages hang in fat strings. Everywhere there is a faint, pleasant smell of smoked ham, so that all that remains is to buy the wine, vodka and champagne.

Caviare Eggs

Pride of place on the *zakuski* table must go to caviare, which in Russia has a curious history. It was the Russians who first persuaded the French to start eating the eggs of the sturgeon, not to discard them. Yet while prices soared for this new delicacy in the West, at the end of the nineteenth century Russians pursued a less exclusive tradition. Roe from the *sevruga*, the *osietr* and even the *beluga* was readily available on medium-priced restaurant menus up to the end of the 1970s. Since then, however, difficult environmental conditions undermining the breeding patterns of the fish, and recent pressures on the Russian economy, have pushed up domestic prices and limited availability except in the immediate caviare-producing area in the Volga delta around Astrakhan.

Russians will often choose today to make their *zakuski* of sparkling orange salmon roe instead. The eggs are larger and more liquid than sturgeon roe and the taste more pungent. Salmon roe is tinned in the Russian Far East and a similar product is available in Europe from the USA.

Hard boil the quantity of eggs required, peel and cut in half lengthways. Pound the yolks with a generous teaspoon each of thick sour cream and a sprinkling of chopped chives or green onion. Pile the mixture back into the eggs and top with a small cluster of the salmon roe.

Ikra iz baklazhanov
AUBERGINE CAVIARE

Vegetables usually appear on the deluxe *zakuski* table mainly as garnishes, but for Russians this is a favourite concoction of what is still an exotic vegetable from the south.

450g/1lb baby aubergines
1–2 onions, peeled
1–2 tablespoons sunflower oil
225g/½lb tomatoes, peeled
  and chopped
salt, pepper
marjoram

1   Wipe the aubergines, remove the stalks and bake in a medium oven (180°C/350°F/gas 4) until soft. When cool, cut in half, scoop out the pulp and set the empty halves in a greased baking dish.
2   Chop the onions finely, soften in the oil and add the tomatoes.
3   To the onion and tomato mixture add the chopped aubergine pulp, the marjoram and seasonings and cook to a thick paste. Fill the halves and return to the oven for 10 minutes. Leave to cool and serve cold.

Smoked Fish

Smoked sprats (*kilki*) from the Baltic coast and
smoked sturgeon from the Russian rivers make
delicious *zakuski* served with rye or white bread.
Russians serve smoked fish with a dish of sour cream
with freshly grated horseradish. Smoked eel and
smoked salmon can be served in the same way.

Ryba farshiravannaya
STUFFED WHOLE FISH

The *pièce de résistance* of the cold table is fish,
either in aspic or, as in this recipe, stuffed with a
forcemeat and garnished.

450g/1lb white fish fillet
1 boned salmon or salmon trout, about 2kg/4½lb
100ml/4floz/½cup milk or sour cream
50g/2oz/¼cup butter
1-2 onions
1 egg, beaten
2-3 tablespoons fresh white breadcrumbs
¼teaspoon each salt, black pepper and cayenne
150ml/6floz/⅔cup sour cream
freshly grated horseradish

1   Gut the white fish. Leave the head in place but
remove the gills and eyes. Cut off the backbone at
the head and tail and discard. Now remove the ribs
and flesh with a very sharp knife, leaving just a thin
layer of skin and flesh.
2   With the salmon and additional fillet, make a
forcemeat by combining with the cream, onion
sautéed in butter, beaten egg and fresh breadcrumbs.
Season well. Stuff the fish, giving it a natural shape.

34

3   Wrap the whole fish tightly in tin foil and bake for
20 minutes in a medium oven (180°C/350°F/gas 4.)
Leave the fish wrapped. Chill for 6-8 hours, then
remove the foil carefully. The skin should come
away too, leaving a perfectly moulded fish with head
and tail intact. Serve garnished with flat parsley,
radishes, tomatoes and other greenery finely
chopped and sprinkled colourfully over the body of
the fish and around it. For the sauce, add 2
teaspoons of freshly grated horseradish to the sour
cream, mix well and serve separately.

Mushrooms Julien

After an array of cold starters this hot titbit a
welcome change of texture. Make it at home in
small ramekins.

2 onions, peeled
1kg/2¼lb fresh button mushrooms, quartered
4 tablespoons butter
2 tablespoons flour
300ml/½pint/1cup sour cream
4 tablespoons grated hard cheese (optional)
freshly ground black pepper
salt to taste

1   Soften the chopped onion in half the butter,
taking care not to brown it.
2   Set the mushrooms on a low heat to release their
juice, then add the remaining butter and the onions
and their juices. When the mushrooms soften,
sprinkle over the flour, cook for a few moments over
a gentle heat, then gently add the sour cream,
stirring. Cook until well blended, add the cheese,
season and bake in ramekins in a preheated oven
(200°C/400°F/gas 6) until a brown crust forms.

Second Courses

Pirozhki
BEEF OR PORK PATTIES

These are small pies made with yeast-leavened pastry, usually filled with meat and served with a clear beef broth.

For the dough:
¼teaspoon dried yeast dissolved in 2 tablespoons of water/milk mixture
400g/14oz/1¾cups flour
1 egg plus 1 for brushing pastry
150ml/6floz/⅔cup water and milk mixed
2tablespoons oil
½teaspoon salt

For the filling:
300g/10oz each minced beef and pork
2 onions, peeled and grated
salt, pepper, nutmeg

1   Mix the yeast mixture, flour, salt and liquid to a smooth dough and leave to rise, covered, for 30 minutes.
2   Roll out to about half a finger thick and cut in circles 7cm/2½in in diameter. Place a teaspoon of filling on each, fold over and press edges to seal.
3   Leave to prove for 30 minutes, brush with beaten egg, prick with a fork and bake in a preheated medium (180°C/350°F/gas 4) oven.

Pelmeni
PASTA IN MUSTARD CREAM SAUCE

Pelmeni are Siberian pasta pouches, smaller than Italian ravioli and made with a pasta dough low in eggs. Unlike many Russian dishes *pelmeni* served with a sour cream sauce go well with red wine.

For the dough:
400g/14oz/1¾cups flour or more as required
125ml/¼pint/½cup milk
1 egg
pinch of salt
1teaspoon sunflower oil

For the filling:
see *pirozhki* (p.36)

For the sauce:
130ml/5floz/½cup sour cream
1teaspoon flour
1-2teaspoons made mustard

1   Make the dough, adding the oil last. Roll out thinly, otherwise cut and fill as for *pirozhki*, sealing well. Bring a large pan of salted water to the boil, reduce to simmering and add the *pelmeni*, which are cooked when they rise to the surface.
2   Drain well. Mix a spoonful of cream into the flour, add to the remaining cream and mustard in a small pan and gently heat through.
3   Either pour over the *pelmeni* or add these to the sauce in the pan, making sure they are well coated before serving.

Main Courses

These consist mainly of roast, grilled or traditionally boiled meats.

Shashlyk

1kg/2¼lb lean lamb, cubed
salt and black pepper to taste
2 tablespoons vinegar or lemon juice
1 onion, finely chopped
1-2 tablespoons oil

For the garnish:
spring onions, pickled cucumbers, tomatoes, lemon wedges

1   Season the lamb well in a large bowl, stir in the vinegar and onion and marinate for 2-3 hours. Remove from the marinade, brush with oil and grill or barbecue.
2   Serve with a generous garnish of raw vegetables and boiled rice.

Roast Duck with Apples

1 roasting duck about 2kg/4½lb
450g/1lb apples
180g/6oz/1cup buckwheat groats

1   Roast the duck in your favourite way. Serve with its own gravy and apples, halved, cored, sprinkled with sugar and baked until soft. Buckwheat *kasha* (p.59) would go well with this dish.

38

The Sweet Course

Morozhennoe
RUSSIAN ICE CREAM

The year-round Russian love of ice cream rivals that of the United States and Italy. Ice cream is ideally served with fresh berries in season from the forest – whortleberries, blueberries, cranberries, boysenberries – and for a special occasion with a glass of sweet sparkling wine or 'Russian champagne'.

Slivochny plombir
CREAMY ICE-CREAM

600ml/1pint/2½cups double cream
300ml/½pint/1cup single cream or milk
5 egg yolks
180g/6oz/¾cup sugar
2teaspoons vanilla essence or a vanilla pod
125–250g/4–8oz chopped glacé fruits (optional)

1   Cream together sugar and egg yolks until white. Stir in the single cream or milk and, having added the vanilla pod or essence, heat gently in a stainless steel pan, stirring continuously, until the sugar dissolves and the mixture thickens. Remove the vanilla pod and chill till half-frozen.
2   Add the double cream and the glacé fruits if required; beat well and refreeze.

This rich ice cream is best removed from the freezer 5 to 10 minutes before serving, depending on room temperature. Top with berries, homemade *varenye* (see p.53) or a fruit syrup or liqueur.

The Russian Hearth
and
Home Entertaining

The traditional Russian welcome to guests is bread and salt. *Khlebosolstvo* was a literal ritual in ancient Russia, when the table was covered with a white cloth, and bread placed upon it the whole day, as a sign that any guest was welcome. Into early modern times, at a private celebratory meal, once the guests were formally seated at the table under the icons, the host would hand every diner a piece of bread sprinkled with salt as a sign of his respect. Afterwards the meal would begin with a succession of individually served dishes, according to the means of the household.

The bread was baked in the traditional stove, round which the family gathered, and which stood as another sign of welcome, as well as providing a warm place to sleep.

Today Russians will still always produce bread, vodka and pickles for an unexpected guest.

Rzhanoi khleb
RYE BREAD

This is a simple recipe for all-rye bread. Since rye is low in gluten, the result is heavy, but the taste incomparable.

500g/1lb/2cups rye flour
½teaspoon salt
½teaspoon dried yeast
125–150ml/4–6floz/½–⅔cup water
2tablespoons sunflower oil
2 eggs

1   Sieve the flour and salt. Add the yeast to just warm water and allow to dissolve. When bubbles appear stir the mixture, combine with the flour, oil and eggs, kneading until smooth. Since rye is hard to work the job is best done with a food processor or mixer. The finished dough may still be slightly sticky, but resist the temptation to add more flour.
2   Leave to rise wrapped in a plastic bag in a warm place, preferably overnight. Bake in a preheated oven (180°C/350°F/gas 4) for about 30 minutes.
3   Cool on a rack and eat fresh, sliced thinly, with homemade pickles, vodka and smoked fish.

Griby marinovannye
MARINATED MUSHROOMS

Pickled or marinated mushrooms have a special
luxuriousness. They also add a new dimension to
drinking vodka.

600ml/1pint/2½cups wine vinegar
1 bay leaf
peppercorns, fennel or dill seeds,
  a dried chilli pepper, a clove
450g/1lb button mushrooms
sunflower oil

1 Bring the vinegar and spices to the boil and allow
to cool.
2 Wipe the mushrooms clean. Bring them to the
boil in salted water, drain and put in a storage jar.
Pour over the spiced vinegar, seal with a layer of
sunflower oil. Leave for a few weeks to mature in a
cool dark place. Use as you would pickled onions.

Ogurtsy marinovannye
PICKLED CUCUMBERS

The cucumbers should be the short ridge variety,
nowadays available in the West all year round, and
they should be pickled very crisp and fresh.

2tablespoons wine vinegar
1–2tablespoons vodka
1.1litres/1¾pints/4½cups water
6 cucumbers, rinsed in cold water and wiped dry
garlic, dill, 1–2 red chillis
1½teaspoons salt

Combine the liquid marinade ingredients, bring to
just below boiling and pour over the cucumbers and
spices to cover in a jar with a tight-fitting lid. Make
sure the cucumbers are covered and top up with
cold marinade next day if necessary. Keep in a cool
dark place for a few weeks.

Pirogi

PIES

Russian pies are legendary, having been central features of banquets since the Middle Ages. Their elaborate preparation celebrates birthdays, diplomatic visits, state anniversaries.

Kurnik

CHICKEN PIE

Chicken is a symbol of fertility, which suggests why chicken pie is traditional at the wedding breakfast.

For the dough:
1tablespoon sugar
¼pint warm milk
510g/18oz/2¼cups unbleached white flour
3tablespoons butter
½teaspoon baking powder
2tablespoons sour cream
¼teaspoon pinch of salt

For the pancakes (6):
180g/6oz/¾cup white flour
2 scant teaspoons sugar
1 egg
200ml/8floz/1cup milk
¼teaspoon salt

1st filling:
50g/2oz/½cup rice (uncooked weight)
2 chopped spring onions, including green part
1–2tablespoons fresh dill, chopped
1tablespoon sunflower oil
1 hard-boiled egg, peeled and diced
generous pinch of salt

2nd filling:
450g/1lb chicken
2 tablespoons oil
1 teaspoon flour
125ml/¼pint/½cup rich chicken stock

3rd filling:
180g/6oz/1½cups fresh mushrooms
1 tablespoon butter
1 teaspoon flour
2 tablespoons sour cream
salt and pepper to taste
beaten egg to brush pastry

1   Simmer the chicken in stock or water. Set the rice to cook in salted water.
2   Mix together the pancake ingredients and bake six small pancakes (about 12cm/5in in diameter), adding a few drops of oil to the pan for each new pancake.
3   Meanwhile assemble the dough by dissolving the sugar in the warm milk and adding the flour in two equal quantities, with second time round all the remaining ingredients. Knead well to form a smooth dough.

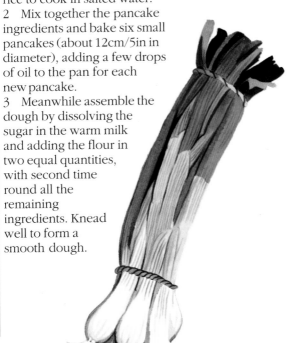

4   *To make the 1st filling*: drain the rice and allow to cool. Add the chopped greenery, oil, hard-boiled egg and salt.

5   *To make the 2nd filling*: drain and dice the cooked chicken if taken from a whole bird. Transfer to a frying pan with the oil and fry lightly. Sprinkle over the flour, cook for 2 minutes and add the stock, stirring till the mixture thickens. It should be a moist consistency, but not so it will run out of the pie.

6   *To make the 3rd filling*: wipe the mushrooms clean, quarter them and begin cooking in a dry pan, then, when they yield their juice, add the butter. Dust with flour and cook for 2 minutes. Finish with the sour cream and season lightly.

7   Divide the dough in two. Roll out the first section to an oval about 30cm/12in in diameter, to fit your baking tray. Grease and flour the tray ahead of time. The dough should be just less than a finger thick. Line it with 2 whole pancakes. Over this surface spread first half the rice mixture, then 2 more pancakes, then the chicken, the mushrooms and finish with the rice. Top the whole with the remaining pancakes. Roll out the second half of the pastry to an oval large enough to cover the filling easily. The finished pie should be shaped like a cupola serving dish. Trim any excess pastry at the foot of the pie, press the edges together and decorate with a fork.

8   Excess pastry can be used to decorate the body of the pie, which should be pricked in 3 or 4 places and brushed with beaten egg before baking for about 30 minutes in a pre-heated oven at 180°C/350°F/gas 4, with a further 10 minutes at 160°C/325°F/gas 3. The pastry should be crisp and golden, with a biscuity but not hard texture.

Kulebyaka
FISH PIE

French chefs working in Russia in the nineteenth century saw the potential in this naturally most luxurious of Russian pie recipes. Where in Russia pike (*shchuka*) would often have been used, a suitable substitute today is turbot or halibut.

For the dough:
½teaspoon dried yeast
300ml/½pint/1cup warm milk
600g/1lb 5oz/2¾cups bread flour
pinch of salt
50g/2oz butter
2 egg yolks

1st filling:
400g/14oz halibut or turbot fillet
1tablespoon sunflower oil
2 hardboiled eggs
2tablespoons fresh breadcrumbs
1tablespoon sour cream
100ml/4floz/½cup milk
1 medium onion, finely chopped
½teaspoon salt
freshly ground black pepper

2nd filling:
100g/4oz/1cup rice
1tablespoon sunflower or other vegetable oil
½teaspoon salt

3rd filling:
300g/10oz halibut or turbot fillet
beaten egg to brush pastry

1   *To make the dough:* dissolve the yeast and sugar in the warm milk. Add the flour, salt, butter and egg yolks and knead to smooth dough. Cover with an oiled plastic bag and leave to rise.

2   *To make the 2nd filling:* cook the rice in salted water until just tender. Drain and dry off a little in a warm oven and pour over the oil.

3   *To make the 1st filling:* combine all the ingredients except the hardboiled eggs. This filling can be made very smooth in a food processor, or the onion and liquid ingredients liquidised then added to the chopped fish and breadcrumbs and chopped eggs, to give a rougher texture.

4   Mix the rice with the oil, and mix with the fish mixture. Roll out the raised dough on a floured surface to give an oval about 35cm/14in. in diameter, or to fit the available baking sheet, which if it is metal should be lined with baking foil. The dough will be about a finger thick. Begin with a layer of rice and fish mixture, lay over it half the filleted fish, then top with the remaining mixture. Lift the short end of the *kulebyaka* towards the top of the pie, raise the two long sides and secure in a top seam. Leave to rise for half an hour in a warm place, prick in several places with a fork, brush with egg, and bake in a preheated oven as for *kurnik* (p.47). The pie is done when a skewer emerges clean.

Pryanik
SPICE CAKE

The Volga town of Gorodets is still famous for its *pryanik* or spice cakes, which used to be sold at the summer Nizhny Novgorod Fair and given as a holiday present to family and friends. Like the finely worked linen tablecloths and wooden utensils painted in the *khokhloma* style, the carved wooden moulds used for this long-lived gingerbread brought together peasant craftsmanship and a traditional culinary speciality.

200g/7oz honey
200g/7oz butter
100g/3½oz/½cup sugar
¼teaspoon salt
2teaspoons cinnamon, ginger, powdered cloves
2 small eggs, beaten
grated rind of ½ lemon
400g/14oz/1¾cups strong plain flour

1   Combine the honey and butter in a saucepan. When the butter has melted remove from the heat, add the sugar, salt, spices and beaten eggs, plus the lemon rind.
2   Gradually work in the flour to make a smooth dough. Roll out thickly on a floured board, cut into decorative shapes with a knife or cutter and bake on a greased and floured baking sheet in a slow oven (140°C/300°F/gas 2).

Chai
TEA

Russia has a tea ceremony in all but name, which both recalls its oriental heritage and suggests an interesting parallel with England, where the fashion for drinking the Chinese brew caught on at the same time, around the mid-seventeenth century. Diplomats brought it back to Moscow as a gift from the Mongolian court.

Truly 'Russian' black tea comes from the now independent Caucasian countries of Georgia and Azerbaidjan and from the Krasnodar region in South Russia, close to the Black Sea. Russian Caravan tea nowadays comes from India and Sri Lanka, or is a blend of Georgian and Indian teas.

Lovely metal tea-glass holders, porcelain and above all samovars have greatly enhanced Russian tea drinking. Samovars or 'self-boiling vessels' originated as forms of thermos to sell hot drinks made of honey and spices called *sbiten*. An internal pipe in the samovar contained hot coals. A tap allowed the drink to be dispensed. With the rise in popularity of tea a fantastic variety of cylindrical, conical and round forms appeared. Samovars were sold by weight and for the tune they sang when the water boiled. The pot containing the strong brew sat on top, waiting to be diluted.

Recipe books suggest milk and cream, but mostly tea in Russia is drunk black, all through the day, and during or after meals. Those who like it sweet drink the amber liquid through an oblong of sugar, rather than dissolving the sugar in the glass. Others commonly take their tea, and above all offer it to guests, with homemade jam (*varenye,* p.52) or fresh raspberries in season.

Fruit Preserves
Varenye

The principle is to produce a strongly-flavoured syrup in which the fruit can retain its natural form. *Varenye* must be something to look at, as much as something to eat, for it is also a memory of summer days at the *dacha*.

Varenye iz zheltykh sliv
RUSSIAN GREENGAGE JAM

For each 1kg/2¼lb of firm greengages:
1.5kg/2¾lb sugar
600ml/1pint/2½cups water

1   Boil a syrup of the sugar and water, add the well-washed greengages and leave to stand for 24 hours. Drain the syrup, boil up and pour over the fruit.
2   On the third day gently cook the fruit in the syrup until tender and a drop of jam sets on a cold plate. Bottle in sterilized jars.

Note: this jam contains stones.

Varenye iz chornoi smorodiny
RUSSIAN BLACKCURRANT JAM

For each 1kg/2¼lbs of blackcurrants:
1kg/2¼lb sugar
600ml/1pint/2½cups water

1   Remove stalks and berry heads from the blackcurrants, wash carefully and drain.
2   Boil up a syrup of the sugar and water, add the berries, bring to the boil and cook gently for about 40 minutes. The berries should remain whole.
3   Test for readiness with a drop of jam on a cold saucer. Bottle immediately in sterilized jars.

National Achievements

Gurievskaya kasha

The most elaborate of Russian puddings, named after a nineteenth-century Finance Minister, Count Guriev, is considered to celebrate Russia's 1812 victory over Napoleon. It was probably the creation of a serf cook which caught the imagination of well-to-do Moscow families.

10 dried apricots
600ml/1pint/2½cups milk
salt
100g/4oz/½cup semolina
2tablespoons sugar
2 eggs, separated
100g/3½oz/1cup chopped walnuts
2tablespoons butter
½teaspoon vanilla essence

1   Soak the apricots in warm water until soft, then chop in quarters.
2   Stir the milk into the semolina in a saucepan, add salt and slowly bring to the boil and allow to thicken. Leave to cool for 5–10 minutes.
3   Meanwhile cream together the sugar and egg yolks, and whisk the white stiff. Toss the nuts in half the butter in a frying pan. Add the yolk and sugar, then the whites to the *kasha*, stir in the nuts and apricots, reserving a few for decoration.
4   Transfer to a greased mould and bake, dotted with the remaining butter. Serve cold decorated with the remaining nuts and fruit.

Shchi

RUSSIAN CABBAGE SOUP

This soup is an eternal source of
Russian vitality and proverbs.

450g/1lb sauerkraut
2 tablespoons tomato purée
2 litres/3½ pints/8½ cups beef or
   mushroom stock
2 tablespoons oil or butter
1 medium onion
1 parsnip
1 tablespoon flour
2 carrots
salt and pepper
fresh parsley, dill, bay leaf
1 clove garlic (optional)
sour cream

1   Drain the sauerkraut, put in a pan
with the tomato purée and enough of
the stock to cover and cook very slowly
for 1-2 hours.
2   Heat the oil in butter in a heavy
bottomed pan and sauté the chopped
vegetables in the oil or butter;
sprinkle with flour, cook for 2
minutes and dilute with the
rest of the stock. Add to the
sauerkraut, plus seasonings,
and cook for 15 minutes
more. Add the herbs in the
last minute and chopped
garlic if liked. Serve with
sour cream.

Mushrooms

Mushroom gathering is a ritual in the autumn. No finer answer exists than the *Boletus edulis* of the Russian forest to those 200 meatless days required by the Church calendar. The mushrooms are used fresh or pickled or salted or dried. The resulting dishes inhabit a world far removed from the strong flavours of Mediterranean mushroom cooking. The best quality mushrooms should be simply sautéed in butter. For humbler varieties, here is an unusual recipe for party buffets.

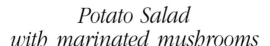

Potato Salad
with marinated mushrooms

2 spring onions
225g/8oz marinated mushrooms (see p.42)
2 medium pickled cucumbers
450g/1lb boiled potatoes
about 125ml/¼pint/⅔cup sunflower oil
2-3tablespoons wine vinegar
1teaspoon sugar
1teaspoon grain mustard (optional)

1   Chop the onions, mushrooms and cucumbers finely. Boil the potatoes and peel if required. Mix all the salad ingredients together and pour over the dressing while the potatoes are still warm.

This salad is delicious with hot sausage or cold smoked ham.

Christmas
Rozhdestvo

The Christmas fast begins on November 28th and lasts until Christmas Day, January 7th. Meat, milk, butter and cheese are all banned, and in the final week fish too. Christmas Eve, January 6th, is still technically modest, but the urge to celebrate it has made much of a simple rice dish. The same *sochevo* is also eaten on Twelfth Night, when a day's fasting returns, on January 18th.

The days in between are meat feasts, when there may be roast goose, and certainly there will be roast pork, which is excellent in this truly Russian combination with buckwheat and cabbage.

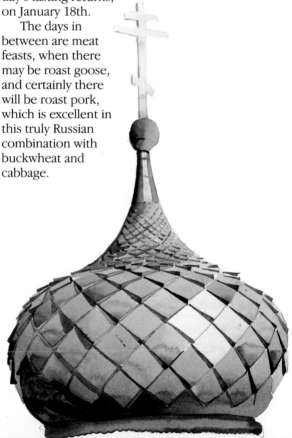

Grechnevaya kasha kapusta tushennaya

ROAST PORK WITH BUCKWHEAT AND CABBAGE

1 Dutch cabbage
2–3 tablespoons sunflower oil
1 onion, chopped
1 well-flavoured apple
1 tablespoon raisins (optional)
½ cup apple juice and ½ cup water
1 small jar of blackcurrants in fruit juice or light syrup
1 roasting joint of pork
180g/6oz buckwheat groats
a bit less than 300ml/½pint/1cup water
salt

1 Prepare the cabbage, which will benefit from long slow cooking and reheating. Heat the oil gently in a heavy stainless steel pan and add the finely chopped raw cabbage and onion. Stir frequently to coat all the vegetables, season, and cook for 5 minutes uncovered. Add the chopped apple, raisins, apple juice and as much water again, cover and stew on the lowest possible heat. If the cabbage seems likely to stick, add a little water. Some blackcurrant juice may also be added.

2 On the day of the meal sprinkle the pork with salt and bake in a pre-heated medium oven (180°C/350°F/gas 4) till crisp on the outside and tender throughout. The meat will need 30-35 minutes per 500g/1lb.

3 Meanwhile prepare the buckwheat. If it is not pre-roasted, heat a heavy- bottomed pan dry over a low heat, add the groats and stir with a wooden spoon until they darken to a deep chestnut. When required cook the roasted groats in a deeper pan with water for about 15 minutes. Stir frequently. Keep back

about a quarter of the water and add it gradually as needed. The *kasha* should be soft but not waterlogged.

4 Serve the pork garnished with the drained blackcurrants, the *kasha* and the cabbage. Vodka complements this rich dish.

Sochelnitskaya kutya or *sochevo*

The ecclesiastical name for Chrismas Eve is *rozhdestvenny sochelnik,* and for Twelfth Night, the Eve of Epiphany, *kreshchensky sochelnik.* The traditional pudding has relatives in Poland, in the funeral and festival wheat and rice puddings of South East Europe and the Middle East, and also in the Christmas porridge of Scandinavia. The custom in Russia dates back to pagan times, when the dish was made of barley or barley and millet.

4 tablespoons pudding rice
600ml/1pint/2½cups almond milk
2 tablespoons sugar or honey
2-3 tablespoons raisins

Put all the ingredients in a greased dish and bake in a medium oven (180°C/350°F/gas4) for 35 minutes. Serve hot or cold.